IN FOCUS

INTELLIGENT ANIMALS

KINGFISHER
LONDON & NEW YORK

Distributed in the U.S. and Canada by Macmillan,
175 Fifth Ave., New York, NY 10010

Library of Congress Cataloging-in-Publication data has been applied for.

Series editor: Hayley Down
Designer: Jeni Child

ISBN (PB): 978-0-7534-7388-7
ISBN (HB): 978-0-7534-7387-0

Kingfisher books are available for special promotions
and premiums. For details contact: Special Markets
Department, Macmillan, 175 Fifth Ave.,
New York, NY 10010.

For more information, please visit
www.kingfisherbooks.com

Printed in China

9 8 7 6 5 4 3 2 1

1TR/0916/WKT/UG/128GSM

Picture credits
The Publisher would like to thank the following for permission to reproduce their material.
Top = t; Bottom = b; Middle = m; Left = l; Right = r
Front cover: iStock/davidevison; Back cover: iStock/clintspencer; Cover flap: iStock/ erhandayi; Page 1 Shutterstock/Paul Hampton; 3 iStock/isuaneye; 4–5 iStock/jag_cz; 4m iStock/zsv3207, 4b Shutterstock/Rudmer Zwerver; 5t iStock/Shongololo90, 5b iStock markrhiggins; 6 iStock/RyanDeanMorrison; 7t iStock/ezeePics Studio, 7b iStock/abzerit; 8–9 Getty/Luis Castaneda; 10–11 iStock/zsv3207, 10b iStock/Konrad Wothe/Minden Pictures, 11t iStock/TheSP4NISH, 11b Alamy/Km Petersen; 12 (1) Alamy/Waterframe, 13 (2) Nature Picture Library/Jane Burton, 13 (3) iStock/Zoran Kolundija, 13 (4) Shutterstock/Andrew Korson, 13 (5) Alamy/Adriane Van Zandbergen, 13 (6) iStock/Ezumeimages, 13 (7) Alamy/blickwinkel, 13 (8) Getty/Richard Du Toit, 13 (9) Alamy/imageBROKER, 13 (10) Shutterstock/Reptiles4all; 14t Alamy/AndyHammer, 14m Creative Commons; 15t Alamy/blickwinkel, 15m iStock/Uwe bergwitz; 16–17 Getty/Jim Abernethy, 16b Shuterstock. kudla, 17m iStock/Snowleopard1; 18 Alamy/ARCTIC IMAGES; 19t Alamy/B. A. E. Inc., 19b iStoc/gmcoop; 20–21 Alamy/GM Photo Images; 22t Shutterstock/Ryan M. Bolton, 22bl Getty/The Washington Post, 22br Alamy/Nature Picture Library; 23t Alamy/Worldfptp, 23bl Alamy/Paul Oliviera, 23br Alamy/Arterra Picture Library; 24–25 iStock/Eel_Tony; 26–27 Alamy/blickwinkel, 27t iStock/steveo73, 28b iStock/jez_bennett; 29t iStock/JasonPrince, 29m iStock/Utopia_88, 29b iStock/jez_bennett; 30 (1) iStock/Tammy616; 31 (2) iStock/GP232, 31 (3) iStock/kojihirano, 31 (4) iStock/hphimagelibrary, 31 (5) Shutterstock/Edwin Butter, 31 (6) Shutterstock/Rudmer Zwerver, 31 (7) iStock/mariusz_prusacyk, 31 (8) iStock/truog, 31 (9) Alamy/Rolf Nussbaumer Photography, 31 (10) Alamy/Cultura RM; 32–33 Getty/Wayne Lynch; 34–35 iStock/worakit; 36 Getty/Anup Shah; 37t iStock/ANDREYGUDOV, 37b Alamy/Sergey Uryadnikov; 38–39 Alamy/robertharding, 39t iStock/PinkPython, 39b ALamy/Shotshop GmbH; 40–41 Alamy/National Geographic Creative; 42t Shutterstock/Andrew Astbury, 42bl iStock/MivPiv, 42br iStock/BirdImages; 43t iStock/milehightraveler, 43bliStock/kjekol. 43br Alamy/Barbara Gardener; 45t iStock/Kerrick, 45m Alamy/Arterra Picture Library, 45b iStock/thatreec; 46 (1) Getty/Suzi Esterhas; 47 (2) iStock/dptro, 47 (3) iStock/Yann-HUBERT, 47 (4) iStock/jonathonfilskov-photography, 47 (5) iStock/nikamata, 47 (6) iStock/JohnPitcher, 47 (7) iStock/Shonogolo90, 47 (8) Alamy/imagesBROKER, 47 (9) Shutterstock/gilkop, 47 (10) Shutterstock/Katherine Bennett; 48–49 Alamy/Minden Pictures; 50 Alamy/Nature picture Library; 51t iStock/GomezDavid, 51m iStock/markrhiggins, 51b Alamy/ Auscape International Pty Ltd; 52tl iStock/Olesya22, 52tr iStock/GlobalP, 52bl Shutterstock/sakavichanka, 52br Shutterstock/Dmitry Kalinovsky; 53t iStock/CraigRJD, 53bl Shutterstock/StudioSmart, 53br Shutterstock/Glass and Nature; 54–55 iStock/GP232, 55 Shutterstock/Carolina Stratico; 56–57 Getty/Gunter Ziesler; 58 (1)iStock/Photocech; 52 (2) iStock/KenCanning, 52 (3) iStock/pjmalsbury, 52 (4) Alamy/Minden Pictures, 52 (5) iStock/ANDREYGUDKOV, 52 (6) iStock/jeanro, 52 (7) Alamy/dpa picture alliance, 52 (8) iStock/Uwe-Bergwitz, 52 (9) iStock/NEALITPMCCLIMON, 52 (10) iStock/eco2drew; 60 iStock/OlgaLIS; 61 iStock/darios44; 62 iStock/SeanPavonePhoto; 63 iStock/suefeldberg.

IN FOCUS

INTELLIGENT ANIMALS

BY CAMILLA DE LA BEDOYERE

KINGFISHER
NEW YORK

CONTENTS

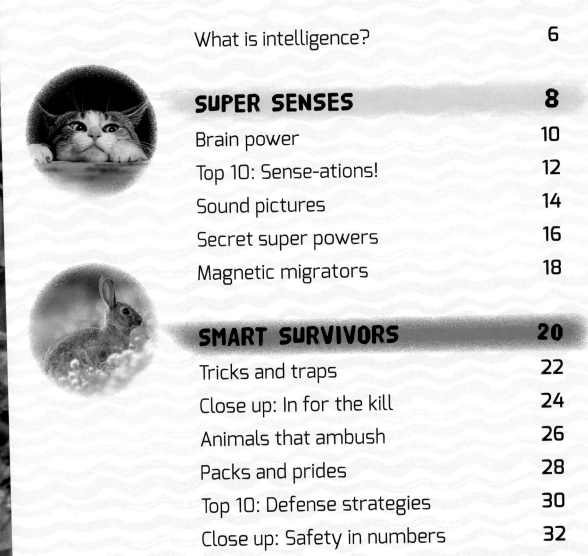

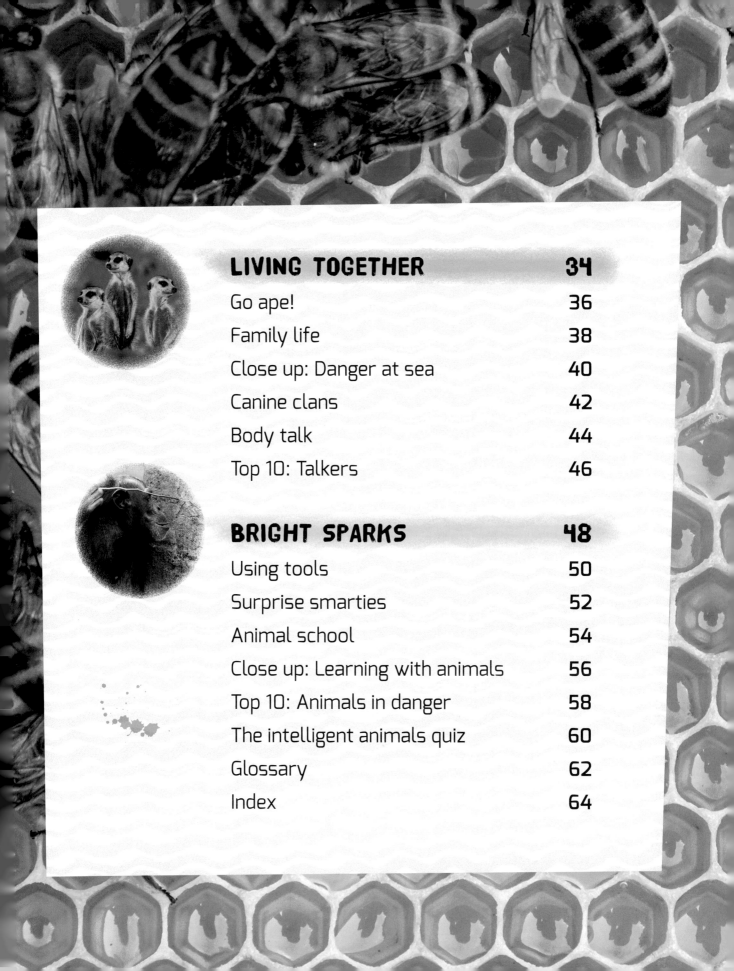

WHAT IS INTELLIGENCE?

How can we figure out how smart animals are, when we are still trying to understand human **intelligence**? That's a question that scientists have been puzzling over for a long time. Deciding what makes an animal "smart" is one problem, but measuring that smartness is just as tricky!

We can never get inside the head of a parrot or a gorilla, so we don't know how it makes decisions, how it plans, or what it feels. One thing we do know, is that animals are as clever as they need to be to carry out their amazing life stories, some of which you will discover in this book.

red squirrel raiding
bird feeder

INSIDE YOU'LL FIND . . .

. . . animals that learn

Learning means **DISCOVERING** new things, from experience or being taught. Dogs learn commands and chimps learn how to use tools. Orangutans have even learned how to wash with soap by copying people!

Communication means **TALKING** to each other. Animals don't use words in the same way as we do, but they have other ways to communicate. Ring-tailed lemurs use smells, and dolphins use clicks and whistles.

. . . smart talkers

. . . big brains

Brain size matters. Generally, a **BIG BRAIN** in relation to the size of the body suggests an animal is intelligent. Monkeys and apes (including humans) have relatively big brains.

SUPER SENSES

BRAIN POWER

An animal's brain is the place that receives information and controls the body. An animal gets information about its surroundings from its senses. That information is carried by **nerves** to the brain, usually in the animal's head.

The brain controls the way an animal reacts to the information it receives, such as deciding to run away from danger. Generally, intelligent animals have bigger brains that can process the information in a more complex way than "simpler" animals. That means they have more options for how they will react.

instincts

Some REACTIONS are **instinctive**. This means they happen without any learning. All animals are born with instincts, and they are essential for survival.

Male bowerbirds, for example, have an instinct to collect colorful objects and build a beautiful bower to impress females. However, they can learn how and where to find the best decorations.

SMART FACT

Will this hamster sense danger?

invertebrates

An invertebrate is an animal without a **BACKBONE**. This group includes bugs, crabs, and octopuses. Invertebrates have nerves and senses, but not all of them have brains. They rely on instinct to survive and are not often thought of as "intelligent."

vertebrates

Vertebrates are animals with a backbone and a **BRAIN**. They include fish, amphibians, reptiles, birds, and mammals. Thanks to their brain, they are more likely to learn and adapt their behavior to suit new situations. Mammals and birds can learn and communicate in especially impressive ways.

TOP 10

SENSE-ATIONS!

Animals understand the world around them using their **senses**: sight, hearing touch, smell, and taste.

1 Sight: huge eyes

Mantis shrimps are invertebrates with large eyes and incredible vision. They can see colors that are invisible to us and other mammals.

2 Sight: mirrors

Cats, big and small, have a mirror-layer in their eyes that reflects light. It means they can hunt at night when their prey can't see them.

7 Smell: antennae

Antennae are long, sensitive body parts. A male hawkmoth's antennae smell the scent of a female, even if she is far away.

3 Hearing: ears

Good hearing helps a fennec fox find insects burrowing in the desert sand. Big ears help to "catch" sounds.

8 Smell: snout

The long, twitching snout of an elephant shrew is very sensitive to touch and smell. It can detect tiny ants and termites under piles of leaves.

4 Hearing: holes

Drumlike ears behind a female frog's eyes are used to hear the call of a male from more than 0.6 mi (1 km) away.

9 Taste: barbels

A catfish's fleshy whiskers are called barbels, and they sense taste. It's a life-saving skill for a fish that hunts in dark, murky water.

5 Touch: whiskers

The whiskers on a seal's face are useful for sensing touch underwater and the movement of air on land. This helps the seal hunt and avoid danger.

10 Taste: tongue

A snake flicks its tongue to taste the air. It then touches its tongue to the top of its mouth, sending nerve signals to the brain.

6 Touch: hairs

A spider's whole body is covered in super-sensitive hairs that detect vibration and the slightest movement of air.

Which sense-ation is your number one?

SOUND PICTURES

Did you know that animals can use sound to see?

BAT POWERS

Hunting at night is a challenge for most animals. With little more than the moonlight to help them see, nocturnal animals often rely on superb hearing, touch, or smell to find food. Bats, however, use a special sense called **echolocation**, or sonar.

They make high-pitched (ultrasonic) sounds in their throat, but send them out through an oddly-shaped nose instead of through their mouth. The sounds, or clicks, bounce off solid objects, such as insects or trees, and are echoed back to the bat.

Large ears help the bat to hear the echoes. They are used to create a "sound picture," which helps the **predator** fly safely through the darkness and snatch insects out of the air.

SMART FACT

BLOOD-DRINKING VAMPIRE bats have another extra-special sense. They can detect the heat given out by an animal's blood as it flows just beneath the surface of the skin. Yikes!

vampire bat

DOLPHIN TALK

Marine predators may have to travel far through the ocean to find food. Light doesn't pass easily through water, so colors and shapes are not always visible, especially where the water is cloudy.

Dolphins use echolocation to overcome these problems. They make ultrasonic clicks by passing air through "lips" inside their nose to form sounds.

The sounds, or clicks, bounce off the dolphin's skull and pass through a round fatty area, called the "melon." This focuses the clicks into a beam that is directed at fish. When the sounds hit the fish's body, they create echoes that bounce back to the dolphin. Dolphins have big, complex brains, so they can use this information to figure out the size, position, speed, and even type of **prey** they are chasing.

river dolphin

SMART FACT

RIVER DOLPHINS use sonar to find fish in murky, slow-flowing waters. They have very poor eyesight, so they rely totally on their sound-seeing skills to survive in rivers, such as the Amazon.

SECRET SUPER POWERS

Your questions about some stunning skills answered.

Can some fish use electricity?

Yes, some can! Electric eels from the Amazon are the most deadly. They generate electricity in their body and release mega-bolts of shocks in the water. Their prey includes fish and frogs, but these 9.8-ft- (3-m-) long predators produce enough electricity to kill humans.

sensory holes!

Why do sharks have a spotty nose?

A shark's nose is covered with tiny holes, not spots, and they are key to a shark's hunting success. Each hole leads to a sense organ that detects the electricity made by another animal's muscles. A shark can sense tiny amounts of electricity and uses this skill to find prey, even flatfish lying still on the seabed!

Why are snakes so deadly?

Many snakes have **venomous** fangs, but that's not the only reason they are supreme predators. Pit vipers have heat-sensitive organs, called pits, between their eyes and their nostrils, which detect the heat given off by their prey, such as small rodents. That means they can hunt in the dark and find prey that is **camouflaged**.

MAGNETIC MIGRATORS

The Earth's magnetic field is generated by molten rock in its core. We use the magnetic field to find north, south, east, and west— unlike us, migrating animals don't need a compass!

Many birds **MIGRATE**, or travel, huge distances to reach feeding or nesting sites. How they find their way is still a bit of a mystery, but the ability to detect magnetism seems to play an important part in this impressive skill.

Young **MIGRATING** birds tend to follow older, more experienced birds, but they soon learn to look out for—and recognize—useful route-markers, such as mountains and coasts.

Although birds can learn migration routes, they also use instinct. **CUCKOOS** are not raised by their parents, but they still know where and when to migrate.

Scientists have found crystals of **MAGNETITE**—a mineral that is used to make magnets—inside birds' beaks.

ARCTIC TERNS take on one of the world's most incredible migrations—from near the North Pole to the Antarctic and back again. They navigate up to 59,650 mi (96,000 km) in a single year!

TERMITES can also detect Earth's magnetic field. They use it to build their tall, thin mounds with the widest sides facing east and west. The shape helps to control the mound's temperature. The wide parts of the mound catch the sunlight in the morning and evening, keeping the mound warm, but in the scorching-hot afternoon, the sun is high over the narrow roof of the mound and doesn't overheat the termites inside.

Scientists think many other animals, including **RAINBOW TROUT** and **HONEYBEES**, use this remarkable magnetic sense to find their way.

SMART
SURVIVORS

TRICKS

How much intelligence does it take these animals to catch their prey?

ALLIGATOR SNAPPING TURTLE

This beast hides in rivers with opens jaws, waggling a long, red tongue that looks like a worm. Fish and frogs try to eat the "worm," then the turtle lives up to its name and snaps its mouth shut around them! This isn't a planned attack; the turtle acts on instinct. When it feels something in its mouth, its instinct is to snap it shut—with a tasty result!

NET-CASTING SPIDER

Many spiders build complex webs, but net-casting spiders hold a silken web between two legs and cast it, like a net, over their prey. Spiders are more intelligent than many invertebrates, with mini "brains" that are so big they spread into their legs. However, their hunting skills appear to be instinctive, not learned.

in the net

snap, snap, yum, yum!

AND TRAPS

AMAZING ARCHERFISH

Archerfish live underwater, but their prey fly above the water's surface. These fish shoot a jet of water to knock a flying insect out of the air and into the water, where it can be gobbled up. Archerfish act on instinct, but with practice—and by watching other fish fail or succeed—they learn how to get better at hitting fast-moving bugs.

great shot!

HUMPBACK WHALE

When humpback whales make a fishnet out of bubbles, they are using a trick they have learned from other whales. A group of whales blows bubbles of air as they swim in circles around a shoal of fish. The bubble net traps the fish, then the whales swim upwards, mouth open, through the net to eat the fish.

brilliant bubbles

IN FOR THE KILL

Bears are adaptable animals, which means they can change their behavior to suit their needs. Scientists believe this is a sign of considerable intelligence. Brown bears have learned that if they stand in a river, facing downstream, migrating salmon will leap right into their mouth! A successful bear can catch up to 100 salmon every day. Genius!

CLOSE UP

More about bears

Fish is full of protein and fat, which the bear stores in its body to help it survive a long, cold winter when food is scarce. Brown bears hibernate during the coldest weather.

ANIMALS THAT AMBUSH

Your questions answered about how animals use stealth and cunning to kill.

Do animals plan their attacks?

Polar bears know that seals pop their head up through ice holes to breathe. They prepare for a seal's appearance by lying patiently next to a hole for hours at a time. They are planning an attack, which will be over in seconds but which will provide calorie-rich food for the bear and their cubs.

Why are great white sharks so scary?

Great white sharks are possibly the most intelligent sharks, and that makes them deadly. They swim in deep, dark water, where their victims can't see them and then, when the time is right, launch into a fast swim upwards, jaws wide open. Their prey (usually a seal) is taken by surprise and has no time to swim to safety.

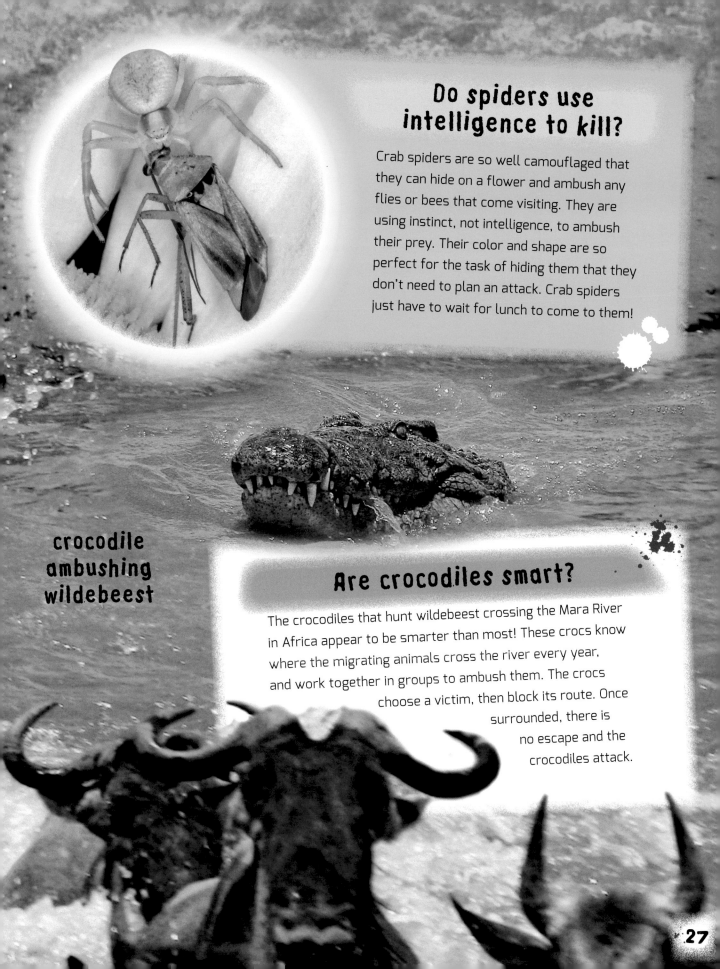

Do spiders use intelligence to kill?

Crab spiders are so well camouflaged that they can hide on a flower and ambush any flies or bees that come visiting. They are using instinct, not intelligence, to ambush their prey. Their color and shape are so perfect for the task of hiding them that they don't need to plan an attack. Crab spiders just have to wait for lunch to come to them!

crocodile ambushing wildebeest

Are crocodiles smart?

The crocodiles that hunt wildebeest crossing the Mara River in Africa appear to be smarter than most! These crocs know where the migrating animals cross the river every year, and work together in groups to ambush them. The crocs choose a victim, then block its route. Once surrounded, there is no escape and the crocodiles attack.

PACKS AND PRIDES

Hunting as a group is a smart move when it means you can catch much bigger prey than you could catch by yourself. Here are some incredible predators that have truly mastered the art of teamwork, and use it to deadly effect. They may not be successful every time they hunt, but the rewards are great when they are—just one kill may provide enough food for the whole group. Hunting packs and prides rely on intelligence and communication to succeed. While the adults do the hard work, youngsters watch and learn.

lions attacking
a wildebeest

sharing jobs

LIONESSES work as a team to hunt large animals such as zebras and wildebeest. While the females hunt, the males stay with the cubs. A group of lions is called a pride.

AFRICAN WILD DOGS are supreme hunters that combine speed with pack-power. They spread out to chase their prey, calling with yaps and barks to coordinate their attack.

pack power

smart strategy

SPOTTED HYENAS hunt their prey in packs, which are led by females. They are very intelligent animals, and by working together they can catch a zebra four times the size of one hyena.

TOP 10

DEFENSE STRATEGIES

Instinct, physical traits, or just pure smarts—which defense strategies work best?

1 Clever camouflage

A camouflaged animal uses color and patterns to blend into its surroundings. Look closely—can you spot the seahorse?

2 Blurred lines

A zebra's stripes make it stand out when it's alone. When a zebra runs, or is in a herd, the stripes blur its outline and confuse predators.

7 Warning calls

If a vervet monkey sees an eagle, it calls to its troop to take cover. If it sees a snake, it uses a different call to tell the troop to climb into a tree!

3 Hot spot!

Bees mob hungry hornets that threaten their **colony**. They beat their wings to raise the temperature—until the heat kills the invader!

8 Mimic masters

A mimic octopus can change its appearance in a flash to fool predators. It can take on the colors and shapes of sea snakes, fish, or jellyfish!

4 Black lemurs

Black lemurs chew giant millipedes to make them release **chemicals**. Lemurs paste their fur with the pulp— it's a homemade bug-repellent!

9 Play dead!

When a Virginia opossum is scared, and there's no place to run, it flips over, hangs out its tongue, and pretends to be dead!

5 Take aim!

Some howler monkeys have learned to throw branches from the treetops at predators prowling around the ground below.

10 Stinky spray

Stinky skunks spray nasty smells at their enemies. Striped skunks do headstands, so they can spray farther and more accurately!

6 Danger drums

While rabbits are grazing, some keep a lookout. If they spot a predator, these rabbits thump the ground with their feet to warn their friends.

Which defense strategy is your number one?

SAFETY IN NUMBERS

Musk oxen are huge, shaggy-furred beasts that graze in herds. If they spy a pack of wolves, they move swiftly into an outward-facing circle, keeping their calves safe in the center.

More about herds

Grazing animals, such as musk oxen, zebras, deer, and antelopes, spend hours eating grass. Standing on an open plain leaves these animals vulnerable to attack, but when everyone is keeping an eye out for a predator, there's safety in numbers. Animals that live, feed, or migrate in groups need to be alert to each other's alarm signals. Calls, whistles, tail flashes, and sudden movements all warn other members of the group to flee.

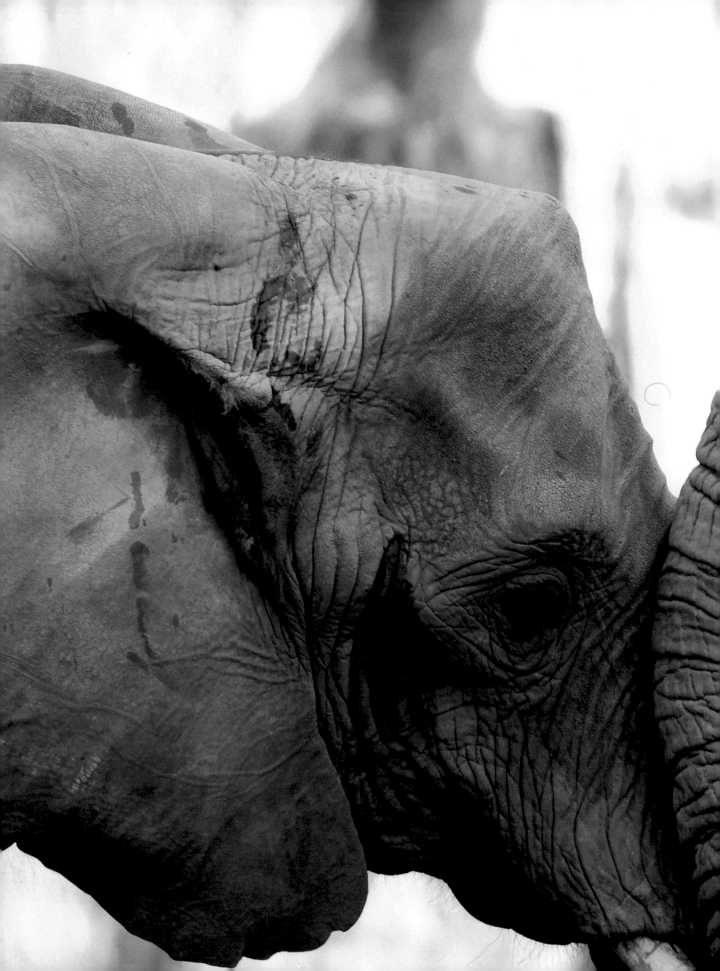

LIVING TOGETHER

When a chimp grins
and shows its teeth, it is
communicating fear or worry—
like a human's nervous smile.
If a chimp glares and opens its
mouth, with its lips over its teeth,
it is warning another
chimp to stay away.

GO APE!

Great apes are our closest relatives. Like us they use tools, live, and work together, and talk and play.

- A **"PANT-HOOT"** is a sound that chimps use to show they are happy or excited. Each chimp has its own pant-hoot, so other members of the family know who's talking, even in a dense, dark jungle.

- Chimps **KISS** to say "hello" and **HUG**, especially when they are feeling scared.

- **ORANGUTANS** make beds from leaves, and they use sticks to get insects out of their holes. Orangutans are fast learners and often learn by copying each other, or humans!

PLAYTIME is an important part of a baby gorilla's day. Apes use play to learn how to live as part of a **GROUP**.

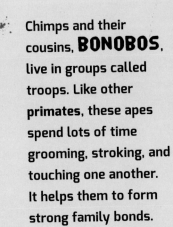

Chimps and their cousins, **BONOBOS**, live in groups called troops. Like other primates, these apes spend lots of time grooming, stroking, and touching one another. It helps them to form strong family bonds.

PARENTS that take care of their families for many years have plenty of time to share knowledge and learning with them.

FAMILY LIFE

Baby elephants need their mothers. But their grandmothers, aunts, siblings, and cousins all help with bringing up baby!

An elephant is one of the few animals that can **RECOGNIZE ITSELF** in a mirror. Most animals ignore their reflection, or think it's another animal.

DAUGHTERS often stay with their mother all their life. When elephants die, the other members of the family have been known to visit the place where the body lay, even years later.

Elephants **STROKE** and caress each other with their trunk. Mothers have been known to smack babies with their trunk!

✱ A group of elephants is called a **HERD**, and is led by the most senior female, called the matriarch. She knows all the best places to find food, and she can remember where to find watering holes.

✱ Elephants **COMMUNICATE** with soft sounds and loud trumpets, but they also make deep rumbles that travel long distances underground. Other elephants feel these rumbles through their feet.

✱ A **BLUE WHALE** is about twenty times the size of an elephant, but its brain is less than twice as big. It's no wonder that elephants are regarded as among the most intelligent creatures on the planet.

✱ An **ANGRY** elephant stares and flaps its ears before it begins to pace. In a split second, it may decide to charge. These are huge, powerful animals with a strong instinct to protect their family.

✱ Elephants **TEACH** their young how to strip sticks from a tree and use them to swat flies away or scratch their back.

DANGER AT SEA

Orcas live in close family groups of about thirty for their entire life. They are nicknamed the "wolves of the sea," because their families, or pods, hunt like a pack of wolves. In this picture, a seal resting on an **ice floe** has no idea that a pod of orcas has decided to target it in an attack. Working together, the orcas create waves that rock the ice floe until it tips—and a final big wave sends the seal sliding down and into the mouth of a waiting orca.

More about orcas

Orcas are large dolphins and, like their smaller cousins,
they have impressive brain power. Younger orcas watch
and learn from a distance. When they are older, they will
know what to do and can join the adults in an attack.

CANINE CLANS

You've probably met a smart pet dog before, but did you know their relatives are intelligent too?

Arctic fox

OUR BEST FRIEND

You probably know that domestic, or pet, dogs can be trained to sit, lie down, and even fetch! But did you know that scientists have discovered the smartest dogs can understand up to 250 human words? Domestic dogs have been bred by humans to have different skills, from hunting to herding sheep.

sheepdog

FOX FAMILIES

Foxes are superb survivors and very adaptable. Thanks to their intelligence they can change their behavior to find and store food for the long winter, and they can live in a range of habitats. Some foxes live in small family groups, in dens, but Arctic foxes usually live alone.

fox and cubs

LONE WOLVES?

Wolves are the **ancestors** of all domestic dogs. They live in groups that are led by one pair of wolves. The adults share the task of taking care of cubs, and they hunt together. They carefully choose their victim before launching an attack and, if necessary, they quickly change their plan during the chase.

wolves in a pack

JACKALS

Jackals usually live in pairs—one male and one female—and mate for life. They share a large territory, which they defend from intruders. Young jackals are allowed to live with their parents until they establish their own territory. Until then, young jackals will help to raise their younger siblings.

homemakers

BODY TALK

Smiles, grimaces, and frowns are three ways in which some animals, such as apes, show their feelings. When an animal uses its body to show its feelings, its behavior is described as "body language." Humans and other apes are expert at it, but so are many other animals . . .

SMART FACT

When an animal **RUBS** its body against a plant, it isn't just scratching an itch—it's spreading its smell around. The smell carries a message, telling other animals to stay away.

stay away!

I'm bored!

SMART FACT

Animals **YAWN**, perhaps to show they are bored or tired. When one animal yawns, others can't stop themselves yawning too!

I give up!

SMART FACT

BATTLES and playtimes often involve a winner and a loser. Dogs show they want to give up by rolling over and exposing their soft belly and throat. The winner backs off, and both animals are saved from injury.

get to work!

SMART FACT

Animals can communicate using smelly chemicals called **PHEROMONES**. Ants use different pheromones to work together to build a nest from leaves, to warn each other when their nest is under attack, or to organize a team to defend the nest.

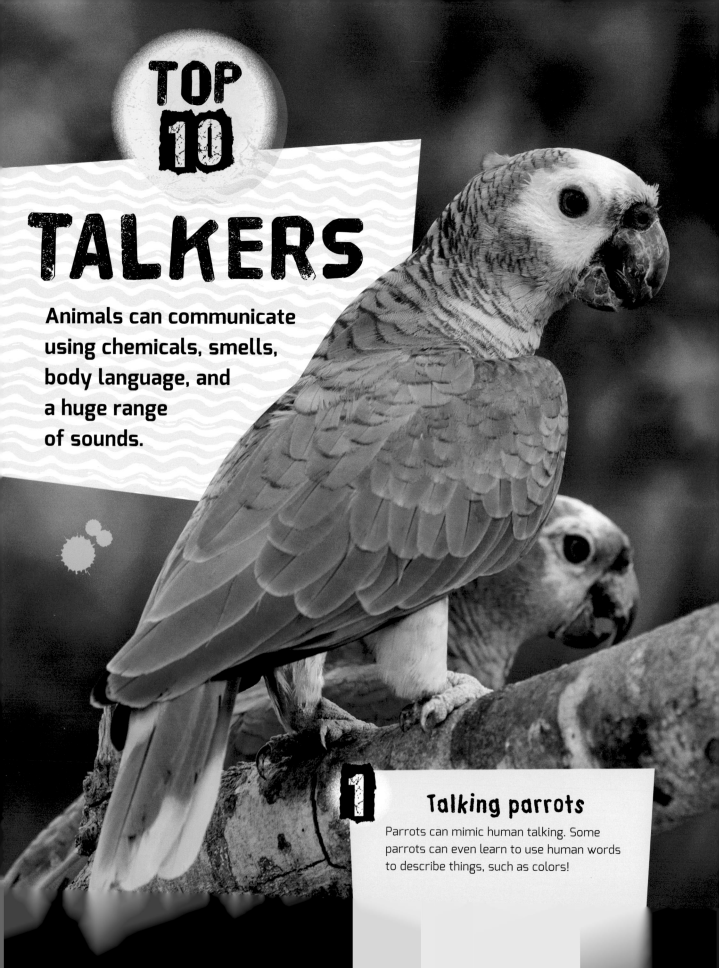

TOP 10

TALKERS

Animals can communicate using chemicals, smells, body language, and a huge range of sounds.

1 Talking parrots

Parrots can mimic human talking. Some parrots can even learn to use human words to describe things, such as colors!

2 Gorilla grunts

Wild gorillas use sound and body language to communicate, but scientists have taught some gorillas to use sign language too.

7 Chit chat

Meerkats purr when they're happy, chatter when they're nervous, and squeal when they spot danger!

3 Whale song

The loudest song is sung by blue whales, but humpback whales sing the longest and most complex songs of any animal.

8 Marsh warbler

This bird can copy other birds' songs, learning up to 100 different tunes that it uses to compose its own melodies.

4 Cuddly critters

A prairie dog uses cuddles and kisses to communicate, but it can also use about ten different barks to tell its family where danger lies.

9 Wet whistlers

A bottlenose dolphin makes its own unique whistle. Scientists think these whistles are used in the same way as we use a name!

5 Grasshopper chirps

A grasshopper communicates with chirps. It makes these loud sounds by rubbing its legs against its wings.

10 Queen calls

When death's head moths enter a beehive to steal honey, they make squeaks similar to those of a queen bee, so the bees ignore them!

6 Coyote calls

A coyote can yip, howl, or bark to its pack. The pack can probably recognize which family member is calling to them.

Which animal would you like to talk to?

USING TOOLS

For a long time, it was thought that humans were the only animals that could make and use tools. In fact, many animals are able to use sticks, stones, and other objects to make life easier. They may learn to use tools by trial and error, or they learn by watching other members of their species. Sometimes, the use of a tool is pure instinct and doesn't need any learning at all.

capuchin monkey

SMART FACT

CAPUCHIN MONKEYS find heavy rocks and smash nuts with them. It's much quicker and easier than trying to crack a nut open with their teeth!

SEA OTTERS collect shellfish and rocks from the seabed. Then, floating on their back, they bash the shellfish with the rock to break it open.

otters rock!

chimp champions

A chimp pushes a stick into a termite mound and pulls it out when it's covered in termites. Chimps also make spears from sticks, which they use to hunt.

CROWS are among the most intelligent birds. They can pick up a stick in their beak and use it to poke food out of a hollow branch. They can even bend wire to make a hook!

clever crow

SURPRISE

RATS

Many **experiments** have been conducted to find out if rats are intelligent. In one experiment, two rats were placed in a pen, one free to roam and the other locked in a cell. The free rat unlocked its friend before eating the food in the pen. This suggests that rats care about each other.

rat race

PIGS

Scientists have been surprised to discover just how smart pigs are! One experiment involved placing food hidden from plain view, but visibly reflected in mirrors around the pen. The pigs were able to use the mirrors to find the food within 23 seconds—easy peasy!

big squeal

SMARTIES

Don't underestimate these animals; they are smarter than you might think . . .

INSECTS

Social insects, such as bees, wasps, ants, and termites, live in colonies with complex social structures. It's common for social insects to leave all the egg-laying to one female, called the queen. Workers care for eggs and larvae and fetch food, while soldiers protect the colony from attack.

clever bees

COCKATOOS

Unlike crows, most birds are not smart enough to make tools. Figaro, a Goffin's cockatoo, is an exception! He sculpted a tool out of wood and used it to pull food from hard-to-reach spots. This amazed scientists, who later discovered that Figaro could teach other cockatoos his new trick!

birdbrain

ANIMAL SCHOOL

Your questions answered about how animals learn.

Can animals count?

They may not understand numbers the same way we do, but some animals do seem to count. Rats, members of the crow family, parrots, and apes all seem to understand ideas about numbers such as quantities, or amounts, including "more" and "fewer."

Why is playtime useful for learning?

Like children, animals, such as lion cubs, can learn by playing. It gives them a chance to practice hunting, running, and climbing—all skills that they need to survive. Clever youngsters like to investigate the world around them. This may help them to develop problem-solving skills.

Do animal parents teach their children?

Some youngsters can learn just by watching their parents, but it appears that some adults take time to show their young what to do. Meerkat adults show their pups how to kill a scorpion and remove its deadly sting before eating it. Orca mothers take their calves to waters where baby gray whales are born, and show the calves how to make their first kill.

Can wild animals help us?

Yes! If you visit Laguna Beach in Brazil, you might spot wild dolphins and local fishermen working side by side to catch fish. The dolphins herd the fish toward the fishermen and signal with their fins when the fishermen should cast their nets. This has been happening for many generations; the dolphins teach their young how to help, keeping the tradition going!

LEARNING WITH ANIMALS

Scientists who want to know how clever animals are, and how they behave, are called **ethologists**. There is so much more to discover about the incredible creatures we share our planet with. It's important we protect animals and save their habitats so they can live their natural life. And while they do that, we can enjoy watching them—and using our brilliant brain power to try and understand their brilliant brain power!

Would you like to study animal behavior?

If you want to find out how intelligent an animal is, how would you create an experiment? An experiment must not harm the animal in any way. Some of the best animal scientists in history have been the ones who are happy to sit and watch animals behaving naturally, and think about what they are doing, and why. So find some time to watch animals. Take photos, draw pictures, and record your observations and what you have learned.

TOP 10

ANIMALS IN DANGER

Many intelligent creatures are in deadly peril and in danger of becoming **extinct**. Humans threaten their survival, but are we smart enough to save them?

1 Tigers

There are fewer than 3200 of these magnificent cats in the wild. People hunt them for their fur, and the tigers face losing their habitat.

2 Elephants

These mighty, incredibly clever beasts are hunted for the ivory in their tusks. All types of elephant are now endangered.

7 Spix's macaw

Macaws and other parrots are taken from the jungle to be sold as pets. Spix's macaws have not been seen in the wild since 2000.

3 African wild dog

Humans hunt this intelligent animal and it is losing its habitat to farmers. There are fewer than 1500 adults left.

8 River dolphins

The Yangtze river dolphin is probably extinct already. River dolphins are threatened by hunting and pollution.

4 Kakapo

Scientists work hard to protect the last 160 or so kakapos—large flightless parrots—on three islands near New Zealand.

9 Amur leopard

This cat's beautiful fur makes it a target for hunters. There are probably no more than 60 of these Amur leopards left in the wild.

5 Great apes

All of our closest ape cousins face an uncertain future, but none more so than mountain gorillas. There are about 880 of them left.

10 Blue whale

Following worldwide hunting, many whales faced extinction. Most hunting is now banned, but blue whales are not out of danger yet.

6 Red wolf

All wild red wolves had died by 1980. Scientists have released captive ones to create a new wild population of just 50 animals.

Which endangered animal is your number one?

THE INTELLIGENT ANIMALS QUIZ

Are you an expert on intelligent animals? Test your knowledge by completing this quiz! When you've answered all of the questions, turn to page 63 to find your score.

 1 Which of these animals is a vertebrate?
a) Dolphin
b) Octopus
c) Spider

 2 Which word means natural behavior that is not learned?
a) Instant
b) Instinct
c) Intelligence

 3 Which of these tool-users doesn't use a stick to get food?
a) Chimp
b) Crow
c) Sea otter

 4 Which animals are described as canines?
a) Bears
b) Cats
c) Dogs

 5 What does a snake use to taste the air?
a) Its brain and its skin
b) Its tongue and its brain
c) Its tongue and its skin

 6 Which animals use echolocation to find their prey?
a) Bats
b) Parrots
c) Rabbits

 7 How many different tunes might a marsh warbler know?
a) More than 1000
b) More than 100
c) Up to 100

 8 Which smart mammals are called "wolves of the sea"?
a) Elephants
b) Orcas
c) Walruses

 9 Arctic terns go on long journeys. What are the journeys called?
a) Mega-flights
b) Migrations
c) Safaris

10 How do animals sense pheromones?
a) Smell
b) Taste
c) Touch

11 Which animal lives in a pride and shares the family's jobs?
a) Jackal
b) Kangaroo
c) Lion

12 What is an egg-laying honeybee called?
a) The Duchess
b) The Mother
c) The Queen

13 Where would you find a barbel?
a) On a fish's chin
b) On a pig's snout
c) On a spider's leg

14 Which type of bear plans its attacks on seals?
a) Grizzly bear
b) Panda bear
c) Polar bear

15 Where do dolphins and fishermen work together?
a) Austria
b) Brazil
c) Zimbabwe

16 Which animal is an invertebrate?
a) Koala
b) Octopus
c) Zebra

17 Which animal has a "melon" in its head?
a) Dolphin
b) Mantis shrimp
c) Tiger

18 Where do crocodiles ambush wildebeest?
a) Africa
b) Australia
c) Europe

19 Which animal teaches its young?
a) Electric eel
b) Elephant
c) Cuckoo

20 Which animal makes bubble nets to catch fish?
a) Catfish
b) Chimpanzee
c) Humpback whale

GLOSSARY

Ancestor
A type of animal or plant that other animals or plants have evolved from. Domestic dogs evolved from wolves, so wolves are their ancestors.

Camouflaged
Describes the way that colors and patterns can help an animal hide or disguise itself against a background.

Chemicals
The substances that make up living and non-living things.

Colony
A group of one type of animal, such as honeybees or ants, that live together.

Communication
The way that animals send and receive information.

Echolocation
A sense used by some animals to discover other objects nearby, using sounds and their echoes.

Ethologist
A scientist who studies animal behavior.

Experiment
To experiment is to test an idea or make a scientific discovery.

Extinct
To have died out and no longer exist.

Great ape
A large, tailless primate. There are four types of great ape: gorillas, chimpanzees, bonobos, and orangutans.

Ice floe
A large piece of floating ice.

Instinctive
Describes a type of behavior that is natural and does not need any learning to happen.

Intelligence
The ways that an animal can adapt, learn, and communicate are just some of the ways we recognize how clever, or intelligent, an animal is.

Primate
Humans, apes, and monkeys are primates. Primates have hands, a big brain, and eyes that face forward.

Sense
The way that an animal receives information about the world. There are five main senses: sight, hearing, touch, smell, and taste.

Venomous
A type of poison that is usually forced into another animal's body by biting or stinging.

Vertebrate
An animal that has a backbone, such as mammals, birds, reptiles, amphibians, and fish.

Invertebrate
An animal without a backbone, such as insects, worms, and spiders.

Magnetic field
Moving metal inside Earth creates a huge area of magnetism around the planet; this is the magnetic field.

Magnetism
A force created by electrical currents that gives magnets their ability to attract and repel.

Migration
A long journey that an animal takes in search of food, water, shelter, or mates.

Nerves
Special cells that carry electrical messages (signals) through an animal's body, providing it with information and instructions.

Pheromones
Chemical messengers that are made by an animal's body and sensed by another animal. Pheromones affect animal behavior.

Predator
An animal that hunts other animals to eat.

Prey
Animals that are hunted by predators.

QUIZ ANSWERS: 1 = a, 2 = b, 3 = c, 4 = c, 5 = b, 6 = a, 7 = c, 8 = b, 9 = b, 10 = a, 11 = c, 12 = c, 13 = a, 14 = c, 15 = b, 16 = b, 17 = a, 18 = a, 19 = b, 20 = c.

INDEX